Learn the Right Way Real Estate

Table of Contents

Preface

Real estate is one of the best investments that anyone can make. Real estate naturally increases in value over time due to several factors so an investment in real property is an easy way to secure your cash flow into the future. Real estate also can be a source of passive income for those looking to devote their free time to other pursuits. Indeed, real estate has become a popular choice of the second career because it can give men and women the financial freedom to live a life free from the constraints of the office. In Learn the Right Way Real Estate, we examine one of the most popular opportunities in this field, property flipping, and learn how flipping the right way can result in capital gains.

Many people enter the real estate business because this industry utilizes skills that anyone can hone with time and the right attitude. Indeed, real estate is what you make of it, and this is just as true of flipping as it is of other forms of real estate investment. In fact, it is important for men and women interested in real estate to understand that this industry is really about investment. Investments of cash in property can lead to rental income collected passively or, in the case of flipping, the capital is returned after a short period due to reselling of the property.

Most forms of real estate investment involve a long-term commitment because cash put into a property in the short term may not see a return for many years. Indeed, a mortgage is a common form of financing a real estate purchase because it allows a buyer or investor to pay off a capital investment over several years (often between 15 and 30). Mortgages are often used for the purchase of private property that is intended for living and not for rental income or resale. Therefore, mortgages and other forms of financing real estate purchases are often used as a type of long-term investment. When one uses a mortgage to purchase a property for rental income or resale, the possibilities for earning income relatively quickly are endless.

This is one of the reasons why flipping has become a popular option for men and women looking to make capital gains quickly. Mortgages and other forms of real estate investment can be used to purchase property that is renovated or improved and resold at a premium. The investment in time in flipping a property is much less than is generally found in real estate. Some buyers and investors interested in flipping choose to purchase property solely with private capital (that is, without obtaining a mortgage or other form of a loan). Although this naturally comes with greater risk as the buyer uses more of their own funds for a purchase, it is common in flipping and is generally less risky than people imagine.

Learn the Right Way Real Estate

Because the idea behind flipping is that property is increased in value by the investment in the structure of the property, most men and women can do well in flipping whether they use their own funds entirely or contract some form of debt.

Naturally, the most successful flippers will have some type of background or knowledge in real estate. Doing well in real estate generally requires the ability to analyze the market in order to make informed decisions about property purchases. It is also critical to understand how to make a risk-benefit analysis in terms of investing in your property. This is especially true in flipping (as opposed to purchasing a home for you to live in) since you expect that your cash investment will lead to a great return.

Fortunately, real estate investing is a subject that is perfectly understandable to most people. Being able to analyze a market to understand where property values are increasing and where values may be stagnant or falling is a skill that most people can develop easily. The real estate market can be volatile, just like other investment markets, including stocks, bonds, commodities, and currency. The real estate market has historically been somewhat less volatile than other markets because housing is a basic need that human beings have so under normal circumstances investing here is relatively safe.

Learn the Right Way Real Estate

Anyone who has followed the real estate market in the last twenty years (or the major world economies during this period) knows that as safe as the real estate market may be compared to other investment markets there is still an element of volatility that has been encapsulated in the form of several real estate's crashes. These crashes have been due to markets that have been artificially inflated in value due to a premium on land and real property. One of the goals of this book is to help you to determine when the properties in a particular area are inflated, which represents a riskier investment.

In Learn the Right Way Real Estate you will learn the skills that you need to be successful in turning over a real property for profit. You will learn how to develop goals and strategies in real estate flipping that are based on an understanding of the real estate market in 2019 as well as an analysis of housing values in a particular area. Many forces can impact property values and it is important to get a feel for this if you plan to flip. For example, property values tend to trend down in areas that are experiencing population shrinkage. Your strategy may include looking at demographic trends in an area as part of your decision to invest there or not.

It is also important to have goals in flipping. Real estate investing is generally a long-term endeavor, but profits from flipping can come much more rapidly than is typically seen in real estate. You will have to think about what your goals are in terms of how involved in flipping you plan to be and how much you are willing to invest. Experienced flippers can be involved in turning over multiple properties at one time while newbies might want to start out with one so they can take it one step at a time. Your flipping goals also involve thinking about how much time you plan on devoting to flipping and whether you are willing (or able) to undertake much of the work yourself.

Having your own team or doing the work yourself can cut flipping costs dramatically.

Many readers will have little or no experience with flipping, renovation, or real estate investing. The best approach to getting started is to be as thoroughly educated on the subject as possible. Books can only take you so far, which is something that readers probably have already guessed. Most of you looking to get started in flipping are already itching at the chance to purchase your first property and turn it over for a profit.

Some of you may have seen televisions shows where professional flippers turn over a property in their area for a tidy profit. These shows may have been the inspiration for you to get started in the business of flipping. But there are some things that it is easy to take for granted in shows like these. These professional flippers are familiar with property values in their area and they know how to choose the best properties. They have teams to aid them in flipping their properties in reasonable amounts of time, and they have a local reputation for ensuring that their property gets sold without a loss. Matters will be a little different for the newbie so in the first chapter, we give you a thorough background to help you develop the best approach to property flipping that you can.

Really, the best approach to any investment is to have a strategy. They tell men and women interested in currency trading to have a strategy and they tell people interested in the stock market to develop a strategy. The same is true for real estate flipping. Indeed, because so much of your success in this business has to do with you - how much money you are willing to put down for a property, how well you are able to flip a property in a given timeline, how aggressively you market the finished property - developing the right strategy may be more important in flipping than in other forms of investment. In the second chapter, you will be provided with the major bullet points and education to allow you to develop the strategy that best suits your flipping goals.

Getting started in flipping will require that you do several things right. Preparation is always an important part of any real estate investment strategy or plan, but it is particularly important in flipping. What you will need to do to get started is to make an analysis of your current work, financial, and time situation. You will also need to have an understanding of what your goals (and needs) are in flipping. If you have a certain amount that you are investing in your projects in any given period, how much capital do you want or need to get back? In addition to capital, you will also need time to engage in your flipping projects, a solid team, and, of course, a strategy. All that you will need to begin flipping properties will be explained in the third chapter.

Although flipping may seem like less of a long-term investment than other real estate investments since most plan to sell (or flip) the property as soon as possible, investors still need to understand that making returns on investment in any form of real estate can take time. It may take longer than you anticipated renovating and selling your project, or you may find that you returned less from the flip than you wanted or needed. Chapter four will help you understand how to incorporate long-term thinking into your short-term flip.

Many men and women have made their fortunes in real estate, from the Hilton and Helmsley families to the Trumps. It may come as a surprise to some, but many of the greats in this industry have experienced just as much failure as success.

Although failure is part of any new endeavor, one of the goals of this book is to help you avoid it as much as possible in order to achieve all the success that flipping can offer. In the fifth chapter, you will learn how the leaders in the real estate industry have used knowledge of market demand, risk-benefit analyses, and other intelligent projections to make great profit in the business.

In order for you to make the sorts of profits that you are looking for in flipping, you will not only have to learn from those that have come before you (forming mentors of a sort), but you will also have to learn from your mistakes. Everyone makes mistakes when getting started in flipping, whether it is in the form of being too ambitious in a project and losing money (or breaking even), or in choosing to invest in an area where the possibilities for profit may be minimal. In the sixth chapter, you will learn about some of the common mistakes that are made in flipping and how you can learn from these to avoid making the same mistakes twice.

Education and planning are important in flipping, but there are also practical concerns about how to finance a project and how much you should put down. Some choose to buy property without going through a bank if they have the means while most will use a mortgage or another form of real estate investment device. In the seventh chapter, we will go over the types of financing that are commonly used in flipping and what options best suit your needs. We will also talk about how if you are unable to flip a property, you may choose instead to earn back your investment through rental income.

Perhaps the most important decision in flipping is which property to choose. Those who have been engaged in flipping for a long time know just what to look for based on the area they are investing in and what their team can turn around in a reasonable period of time. It will be more difficult for readers new in the business to have this six sense of which property to choose to flip over another, but you can develop this sort of intuition over time. In the eighth chapter, we will provide you with the information you need to make an informed property choice. This will entail reviewing the various costs involved in flipping, such as renovation and closing costs.

There are many lessons that can be learned from the successes and failures of pioneers in real estate. If you do not have a tally of successes and failures in your career then that suggests that you never really tried. But the purpose of this book is to steer you in the direction of success. In the ninth chapter, you will be provided with ten major lessons that can be learned about flipping and the real estate industry from the major pioneers in the game. In the last chapter, you will learn the secrets to achieving success in this business. As you will soon learn, with the right approach and a well thought out strategy, success in flipping is not hard to find.

Chapter : 1

Introduction to Real Estate Flipping

The real estate industry can be volatile. Property values can rise precipitously and then quickly fall, making real estate speculation a realm, not for the faint of heart. Indeed, investing in real estate can be a gamble, but like any gamble, the payout is often worth the risk. Perhaps this is what makes investing in this industry so appealing to so many. Most that choose to pursue investments in real estate have a background, but for those who do not, now is the time to get a little education.

Interest rates are an important subject in many areas of investing, not just real estate. Interest rates were being talked about in 2016, 2017, 2018, and will remain an important subject in 2020. The federal government raised interest rates no less than three times in 2018. This is generally seen as a good sign although it did raise a few eyebrows in the industry. As you will see, interest rates should not be the sole deciding factor in your decision to pursue investing in real estate, especially if you are planning to flip.

A rise in interest rates is often interpreted as a sign of a strong economy. Government regulatory agencies often raise interest rates when the economy is strong enough to bear it and they want to curb spending. Interest rates directly impact real estate investing as many buyers obtain mortgages or other types of loans to finance their purchases. As you will see later in this book, you have many options in terms of financing your flips.

Although the role of interest rates in flipping is a little different than it is in other forms of real estate investing, this subject forms a critical introduction to the subject. It is helpful to understand the pattern of interest rate changes and where matters may head in the future. This helps you as a potential flipper (and real estate investor) gets a feel for the industry not unlike those who have been in the game for a long time. Equipped with the basic knowledge of the real estate market and other aspects of flipping that will be key to your future endeavors, you will be ahead of the game in terms of turning a small flipping investment into big profits.

In fact, it is important to remember that real estate is an investment, even flipping. You are putting money into a project and the goal is to make a profit. Although your investment is more of a short-term one than other forms of property investing, it is still an investment. And it is not a passive one. When it comes to flipping, you need to make decisions about what your money is being used for. Yes, your investment dollars are being used as a down payment on a property and for renovations, but which property should you invest in and what sorts of renovations should you take.

Although understanding the real estate market may seem peripheral to the discussion of where to invest your money in a flip, it is, in fact, a central subject. People spend their money differently depending on how the economy is doing, which is a common subject of interest in economics. Luxuries are often the first thing to go when times are hard so it can help to understand what sorts of things are luxuries in the context of a flip. Also, if the economy is doing well these luxuries may be just what you need to seal the deal and secure a hefty profit. Therefore, if you plan to pursue flipping into the future it helps to have an understanding of things like interest rates and market changing.

This is not just true of real estate. Let us say that you have been reading about cryptocurrency and you are considering investing in that arena rather than real estate because of the fortunes that already have been made there in just a few short years. Well, even if you were to pursue cryptocurrency investing as a more suitable investment for your money you would still have to be conscious of economic forces and market factors that impact values in that industry just as much as in a real estate. Indeed, we can say that flipping is relatively straightforward compared to other ways that you may choose to invest your money because there are relatively few areas that require your concentration, Furthermore, the factors at play in property flipping are more likely to be understandable to the average layperson than the equivalent forces involved in currency trading or other comparable investments (in terms of monetary value invested).

Real estate is a good investment and it is a good idea to understand why. Many people regard property as the best investment you can make, and this assessment generally is predicated on the understanding that housing is a basic need that every human being has. Besides, housing values tend to increase over time. Therefore, real estate is often a less risky investment than other investment options, making this particular way of spending (and making) money popular for those who are looking for low risk or who are frightened off by volatile economies. For example, investing in real estate in countries like the United States is very popular for non-US natives looking for an investment safer than what is available at home.

The reality is, most men and women with capital have many options in terms of what to do with their money. Many people choose real estate investing over the other options available to them for just those reasons we mentioned. Of course, it is important to note that though property values tend to rise over time, they do sometimes stagnate or even fall due to economic and demographic factors. In this book,

We hope to give you the tools to tell a good investment from a bad one. We also hope to give you a feel for how flipping is both a part of the general real estate investing world while also being distinct from it.

For those who still need a little convincing on why real estate is a good investment, let us compare it to other investment options. Some individuals may be thinking about investing in a restaurant, but this is an industry that is highly vulnerable to inflation. Remember the discourse we had about populations tending to cut luxury spending during periods of economic hardship. Restaurant food is a luxury. Cryptocurrency is another option because the values of commodities in this area have increased by 100 times or more in a short time. Well, the reader should remember that many regard the cryptocurrency industry as a bubble that will eventually burst. Like paper currency, cryptocurrency has no intrinsic value like gold and other precious metals or food. It is entirely likely that individuals may decide at some point that cryptocurrency is not something that they need and the values of this currency will fall right back to where they started.

But everyone needs shelter, even if it is in the form of a rental unit. The shelter is considered a basic need of mankind right along with food and water. Families all over the world will always need protection from the elements and a warm bed so there will always be a need for shelter as a commodity. In the last days of Communist Eastern Europe, a lack of suitable housing was a complaint that was common in the former Eastern Bloc, representing the reality that the governments of these countries had not fully appreciated how significant acceptable housing was for people's happiness and quality of life.

Real estate is often pursued as a long-term investment as property values tend to increase gradually over time. This gradual increase in property values can be attributed to a number of factors like population increase, economic expansion, increased demand for property, inflation, and other demographic and economic factors. Flipping is a shorter-term investment, but a favorable flipping market is impacted by overall trends in real estate. Therefore, a real estate market that is cooling can be unfavorable for flips because a property that has been purchased and renovated still has to be resold, even if it is only a few weeks or months later.

This is important to understand about flipping because, as you will see later, a newbie in the industry can be misled by low prices or other factors that might entice them to buy. As an example, you may see a 100-year-old property advertised for a price that seems surprisingly low and may be compelled to make the purchase, but this may be a mistake. Old houses may be less sellable in a market that is cooling or where there are many new houses available. Also, Reno work on an old house may be more

Extensive and costly than they would be on a newer property. This is part of the reason why attractive older houses are often priced lower than their apparent value. There are many factors at play in making a property a good investment or a bad one, even in the short-term as is the case with flipping.

Some of you may have information suggesting that the market for real estate is cooling. Cooling in this context simply means that there are fewer people looking to purchase properties so it may be more difficult to find a buyer, which is something that would obviously impact flippers. In particular, there has been a dip in the last few years in the number of new homes constructed. In practical terms, this means that there may be a relative shortage in housing units available for purchase in many areas in the next decade, but it also means property values may see a relative increase in value.

The long and short of it is that you should not allow doom and gloom real estate projections to deter you from pursuing your dream of investing in real estate, especially if you are interested in flipping. There is plenty of money to be made in flipping for the person with the knowledge and capital. Furthermore, things are not quite as gloomy as some information you may have received about the market suggest. Real estate still represents arguably the best investment you can make for your money, especially for those men and women who recognize that time has intrinsic value. Real estate generally leaves investors time to pursue other things, allowing them to get even more bang for their buck.

Think about what most young and middle-aged people do when they get a new job with a hefty sign-on bonus or come into some other form of a cash windfall. They put a down payment on a house. Why?

Because investing in real estate is not only a solid investment, but it represents an investment in your future more so than other types of investments do. Perhaps it is better that you think about flipping as an investment in your future, an investment that will lead to solid returns, one house at a time.

Real Estate Investing as a Source of Income

Real estate investing that you do when you purchase a home should be distinguished from the sort of investing that you do when your goal is income. Most people do not buy their family home because they are looking for income. Investing in this industry can be used for income, which is why a large portion of the millionaires in the United States today have made their fortune in real estate. Investing in a home is one of the most important investments that many people make, but this is not your income stream. You need to see real estate investing as your primary source of income, especially if you plan to flip. In this

Book, you will learn how to choose the right property for you to purchase for flip (or for other purposes if you should have issues selling the property.

Many men and women who invest in real estate use the rental income that they generate to reinvest right back into the market. Their properties, therefore, become a source of regular income that widens over time through the acquisition of property. In addition, you can also increase your net worth simply by the increase in property values over time. This is primarily the case for those using real estate as a source of rental income, but it is also an aspect that potential flippers should keep in mind about the market.

The Real Estate Market Today

Laypeople can be inundated with real estate market news and it can be hard to tell what should be believed and what should be ignored. The news media operates on principles of marketing so they intentionally give you a stark view of events in order to keep you watching. The goal, of course, is to maintain the attention of you, the viewer, and it is easier to do that if the message is that the world is ending because housing values are falling in some part of the country where, in reality, all the people are leaving. It is important to have knowledge of current market factors so you know how to make informed decisions about your money. Indeed, this is one of the main themes of the book.

The reader who understands what is happening in the market today will not be deterred from investing.

The fact is, in spite of the Fed's recent increase in interest rates, the real estate industry is still a great opportunity for investors looking to make capital gains. One of the forces that are important to be knowledgeable of is interest rates. The Fed's increases in interest rates in 2018 means that individuals planning on a mortgage are likely to be met with a higher mortgage payment than what they would otherwise have. Your mortgage payment maybe a couple of hundred dollars higher than in the past, but you also have a larger pool of buyers because of the smaller number of available units. This is why many areas in the United States have seen rents rise dramatically over the last few years. There has even been an increase in the cost of nightly hotel rooms in many areas, and this is all due to housing shortages impacting housing prices, rents, and nightly rates.

So what are some of the trends in the market today that you should keep in mind? In general, these

Include increases in interest rates, a large number of renters and buyers on the market, buyers choosing to rent rather than buy because of fears about the economic downturn, lack of supply of affordable housing, and the drop in the number of new housing units constructed. Also, changing patterns in employment and other economic and demographic patterns are likely to impact the real estate industry.

A drop reduction in new housing units constructed means that there will be a reduction in units available for buyers to purchase. It is true that construction of new units has been rising slowly in the last few years, but this slight uptick is being outpaced by growth in population and the number of buyers on the market looking to purchase. This particular trend has led to increases in housing values in some places, which only muddies the picture further. In places where houses are overpriced because of a lack of available units, the decision of what represents a good or bad investment can be difficult. This is a topic that will be discussed in more detail later.

An increase in individuals looking to rent as well as a lack of affordable housing tends to favor real estate investors planning on creating rental units. In other words, the potential to make money here is not particularly favorable for house flippers. These trends will likely only benefit your flipping endeavor if for some reason you decide to hold on to a property rather than sell it right after you rehabilitated it. In this case, you may be able to charge higher prices for rents than you would otherwise because of the glut of renters, not to mention the improvements in the property that have been made.

The other trends mentioned above contribute to the complex real estate picture that exists today. It should be obvious that even if the rise in interest rates and reports of falling unemployment rates present a favorable economic picture, the reality is perhaps not as straightforward. As the goal is to develop an idea about the real estate market today as a tool in making good flipping decisions it can be said that a general reduction in new housing units tends to favor flipping because of a relative increase in buyers on the market, but it may be wise to exercise a little conservatism when considering investing in markets where a lack of affordable housing units or demographic factors may not favor flipped properties.

Defining Flipping

Flipping properties has been addressed as a type of real estate investment. Flipping is the real estate jargon for purchasing a property and altering it for resale. Altering the property can take the form of superficial changes like a new roof, landscaping, or other exterior work, or it can encompass more involved demolition and renovation work. Properties are referred to as flipped because they are typically resold quickly for a profit rather than holding on to long-term, which typically occur with traditional real estate investment. Speculation in real estate to generate passive income for renting has long been common, although flipping has increased in popularity in the last decade.

The Advantages of Flipping

Property flipping has become popular because there are areas in which it has an advantage over other forms of real estate investment. Indeed, investors, today are looking to get returns on their capital investments quickly rather than hold on to properties for longer periods and generate steady income that accumulates over time. As many investors have this type of goal, flipping presents many advantages vis a vis other forms of real estate investment (and capital investments in general). But this is not the only one. Below is a list of some of the advantages of flipping:

- Flipping is a short-term investment in which returns on capital can be made quickly
- Flipping is usually undertaken in the form of short projects where profit can be made over a period of weeks or months
    - Advanced knowledge of real estate is generally not necessary in flipping
- Because flipping is a shorter-term investment, investors do not have to be concerned about long-term economic changes leading to a drop in property values
- Because properties can occasionally be bought with little money down, the potential to make large profits with flipping is great

- Flipping can leave those involved with free time to pursue other interests
- Flippers can choose where to invest their money in their projects based on their specialized knowledge and essentially function as their own boss
- Profits earned quickly can leave free periods in the year for travel, relaxation, or other forms of employment
- Much of the knowledge required to make money with flipping can be learned quickly

An advanced degree is not needed to achieve success in flipping. Indeed, many of the individuals you hear about in the media who profit in this business do so based solely on the experience they gained through trial and error. In subsequent chapters, you will learn how to get started in flipping, ways that you can finance your purchase, the lessons you can learn from those who have made it in the industry, and how to develop a strategy that can lead you to success in this business.

Chapter : 2

Developing a Flipping Strategy

Developing a strategy is a must for anyone who plans on investing their money wisely. Investing without a strategy truly is a gamble, pulling the lever on the slot machine without a sense of when the dollar signs will align or whether they will align at all. Developing a strategy in real estate allows you to use the forces at work in the industry to your favor. Real estate, like any other industry, is subject to larger factors which can be analyzed and understood. As we have already seen, understanding where the market is today and the factors that have contrived to create this greater market picture allow you to turn risky business into sure profit. If your goal is to be serious about flipping then this is where your motivations should fall.

Anyone can invest dollars into an unknown commodity and hope that they eventually achieve a payout, but most men and women who pursue flipping do not have that goal. The goal of property flippers is generally to take a certain dollar amount, invest it in a property, and obtain a return in a certain period of time, say three months or six months. This type of scheme can be difficult if not impossible when using real estate investment as a form of passive income because of the long-term nature of that type of investment, but it is entirely feasible in flipping.

A strategy is a difference between going into an endeavor blind and having a plan. Losing money is always a risk when you are investing in any kind of market that is subject to forces outside of your control. This is what they teach men and women going into currency trading, and it is just as true of real estate. You can lose your money in flipping (or any other form of real estate investing), but having a strategy makes this possibility much less likely. Indeed, there are many people engaged in flipping who rarely if ever lose capital, and this is primarily due to approaching their endeavors strategically.

What does having a strategy mean in terms of flipping? A flipping strategy is your plan of attack: the process that you use and standardize as part of your goal of making a profit through turning over properties. It is not as involved as you think and it is not as uncommon either. If you watch any of the shows on cable television that involve property sale and resale, they all have a strategy of some sort and the strategies are not always the same. The strategy may be to focus most of the renovation funds on kitchens and bathrooms because these are two of the high-return areas in housing sales. A strategy may be to purchase the ugliest house on the street and make it the most beautiful. Everyone involved in flipping has a strategy of some kind and you will have to develop one too if you plan on making a profit in this industry.

Here we will focus on areas that you should pay attention to in developing your strategy. Although we have focused on a "strategy" as a pragmatic set of practices that guide your behavior in flipping, a strategy also entails the basic things you should do before you get started. For example, you need to understand what your goals are in flipping before you purchase your first property or you might find a year later that your goals are more out of reach now than when you first started. You also need to think about how you can incorporate the realities of the industry into your behavior. You can use market niches and profit gained from property flipping to achieve even greater profits than you ever thought possible.

Creating a Specific Goal

The first step in developing your real estate flipping strategy is creating a specific goal. This is an activity that involves a little self-reflection. This is not someone else dictating to you what you should get out of property flipping and how you should get it. This is you sitting and thinking about why you are flipping and what you need to achieve from flipping in order to be satisfied. At the end of the day, we all would like to feel the satisfaction that comes from striking a balance between our hard work and our natural abilities. This contentment is our highest need and it can be achieved in property flipping by first trying to understand why you are going into flipping in the first place.

Most people are not pursuing flipping as a career because this is what they have always wanted to do ever since they were children. Most people choose to enter this business because they like the idea of real estate and renovation, they have a knack for it, and they are looking to make money with it. Embarking on property flipping for the money is a perfectly acceptable reason to get into this business. Indeed, men and women who are going into flipping because they hope to make a profit relatively quickly and they are clear on this from the beginning are generally more likely to achieve their goal than others who are perhaps less forthright about what their reasons are.

Of course, you can choose to embark on property flipping for reasons that are not primarily centered on finances. Some individuals have a desire to invest in and beautify the communities that they live in. Others see a shortage of high quality, affordable housing in their communities and they hope to rectify the situation by investing their time and money. Because you are dealing with your time and your money, there really is no wrong reason to set off on your flipping journey.

In fact, many people enter this business for more than one reason. This is true of other industries and it is also true of flipping. Perhaps you want to beautify your community, but you also want to make enough money in a six-month period to be able to spend the remaining six months on the beach somewhere. This is a perfectly legitimate goal and an honest one. Goals like these are more likely to result in success because they represent ways in which we can be honest with ourselves and use our energy and talents on paths that align with who we are.

So what you need to do first in developing your flipping strategy is to define what your goals are. Examples may help here to allow readers to get the big picture. Some men and women want to be able to invest in a project and manage it while having time in their day for other things. People like this may have children, maybe in school, or may have other obligations that constrain their time somewhat. Although some people engaged in flipping do not have other engagements, many do. Being clear about this from the beginning – that you have a goal to have a certain amount of time available in your day, week, month, or year – will allow you to act accordingly. In order to accomplish this goal, you may require a partner or team who you can delegate responsibility to rather than micromanaging, but this will all be discussed in time.

Because there is a lot to creating goals in flipping, we have listed below some of the things that you should think about in coming up with your goal(s). Here is a list of some of the things that you should be thinking about:

- List of specific goals in flipping
- List of property types you would like to work with
- List of geographic areas of interest
- List of a general timeline for flipping (e.g. 90-100 days)
- Exploring who will actually do the work
- Exploring whether you will work on one project at a time or multiple projects
- Exploring how much you expect to get back on your investment

This last concept is an important one, one of several in flipping. You should have an idea of an expected return on your investment, or ROI, which will guide your purchases and flipping strategies. This will also help to ensure that you are profitable in flipping. A general rule is to aim for at least a 20% return on your investment. So if you purchase a property for $110,000 and plan to spend $40,000 renovating, that means you have invested a total of $150,000. You should plan to make at least $30,000 in profit, which is 20% of $150,000.

Using Market Niches

Once you have an understanding of the real estate market, you will be able to use market niches to your advantage. Market niches can be thought of as particular types of properties or projects that can generate sales and profit. This also can be thought of as strong points for you that can lead to greater success. For example, if you live in an area where the climate is warm during much of the year and pools are popular, your niche may be to find properties where there are no pool or sliding doors and add these. Or perhaps you are an expert in renovating kitchens affordably so your niche is getting an expensive-looking kitchen into an older house at a fair price.

Your niche can really be anything. Your niche will also be dependent on where you live or plan to work. For example, if you live in the Nevada desert your niche is likely to be different from someone who lives in frosty Upstate New York. Your niche is also going to be impacted by what your areas of experience are and what you can bring to the table. Perhaps you know a place where you can granite for countertops cheaply or affordable hardwood flooring. Of course, not everyone coming into this industry will have an understanding of a niche, but this is something that you can develop over time as you gain more experience.

In addition to a niche being an area of knowledge or strength for you, a niche can also be a type of property that you choose to focus on. You may decide that you want to focus on condos rather than houses, or on beachfront properties, or properties with a lot of acreages. It is not uncommon in real estate for investors and sellers to have a niche. Having a niche allows you to gain a reputation based on an area of strength. It also allows you to be happy in your endeavors by pursuing an area that is satisfying to you.

Using Capital Gains from Flipping

Implied in the term flipping is the idea that this is a process that occurs more than once. Most people who go into property flipping do not plan on investing in a single property, selling it for profit, and then leaving the business for good. Most flippers plan to use the profit that they have gained from flipping to invest in another project and continue on from there.

Men and women who invest in property flipping are able to do this because a well-done flip increases your capital. This is an idea that has been implicit throughout the book if not always explicitly stated. If you invest $300,000 in a project (of which $220,000 was the price of the property and $80,000 was for the renovation) then you would expect to make somewhere close to $350,000 to $400,000 in order to make a healthy profit. Recall that property sales generally include closing costs, fees, taxes, inspections, insurance, and other expenses that make both the purchase of property and the sale often more expensive than we originally expected.

So let us say that you invested somewhere between $300,000 and $310,000 in a flip and you were able to sell the property for $400,000. This means that you not only made back your original capital investment of $300,000 but now have capital of $400,000, representing a gain of $90,000 to $100,000. That gain in the capital can be used to invest in one or more additional flips. The picture becomes more complicated when you take into account how precisely the property was purchased (whether using cash or a mortgage), but that is a subject that will be explored in more detail later.

Now that you have this gain in the capital, you have several options. You can invest in one slightly more expensive property or more than one property. Again, because mortgages are a tool that allows you to acquire property without having to front all of the cash at once, as a flipper you have options available to you in terms of what you choose to do next.

So we can summarize the flipping knowledge of this chapter by saying that a strategy can be developed using several factors, not the least of which is the basic realities of flipping. Knowing that flipping can generate a healthy profit for the successful flipper, you are able to take your goals, your personal knowledge and skill, and your available capital and align them in the form of a strategy. The strategy that results is entire of your own making. If your strategy is to take your capital of $200,000 and invest it in reasonably priced houses that you plan to flip in 6-12 weeks primarily with new kitchens and bathrooms so that you can spend six months of the year on the beach, that is a reasonable strategy that you have aligned with your basic goals.

Most flippers have developed strategies that are much more detailed than this, but this gives you a general idea. Many flippers have a sense of what neighborhoods, towns, or parts of the country they plan to focus on based on market niches and personal knowledge. Others have strategies based on contacts they may have in the industry or their predictions about where the market is likely to head in the future.

Once you have developed a goal and a strategy along these lines, you are ready to begin thinking about getting started in flipping. Getting started involves thinking about what you need to begin in the industry, and how you can go about accomplishing your goals. This process expounds on our initial process of coming up with a strategy by forcing you to further understand your goals and match these with various aspects of the industry.

Chapter : 3

Getting Started in Flipping

Making a beginning in flipping first requires that you understand that you are involving yourself in a type of investment. An investment is, by definition, a means of generating capital or income based on an initial influx of cash. Your goal should be to turn your flipping venture into a good investment. A good investment is one in which a capital gain or profit is made. We can also say that a good investment is one in which the specific goals of the investor are met. As we have already seen, what your goals depend entirely on you.

A good investment should be distinguished from a bad investment. A bad investment is one that is risky, or in which the chances of earning a profit are slim. An example that is often given is investing in restaurants. Restaurants can certainly earn a good deal of profit for their owners and other investors, but a restaurant is essentially a riskier investment than many other investment options, including real estate. When you invest in a rental property, for example, you can be pretty certain that barring any unforeseen circumstances your property will provide you with the income you are inspecting. The same is also true of flips. When all is said and done, most flippers are able to sell their renovated properties, even if it is for less than what they anticipated. With restaurants, it is hard to predict how successful the restaurant will be or if it will achieve any success at all.

We can start off by saying that you are already ahead of the game by choosing to learn more about flipping and investing in educating yourself about the ins and outs of the business. Flipping has become popular because it is not only a good investment generally, but the chances of making capital gains with flipping can be rather high. As with anything else, rewards are generally tied to some effort or know-how. In other words, the individuals who make the most out of flipping tend to be those who put the most effort into their endeavors, acquire the most knowledge, and who know how to use their money wisely.

In order to get started in flipping (aside from the cognitive aspect about understanding what you are getting into) you will need to do several things. Indeed, the steps that you will need to take to begin your career in flipping are not altogether different from the sorts of steps that would be taken in other forms of real estate investing like investing in rental properties. The difference with flipping is that this endeavor can require more capital and your success can be closely tied to the knowledge that you bring in and how much effort you put into the project. Investing in real estate for rental properties can be a hands-off, passive type of endeavor while flipping tends to be more involved. In fact, many flippers choose to directly involve themselves in the property rehab, whether it is putting in new hardwood floors, installing the new kitchen cabinets, putting new coats of paint on the wall, and the like.

The purpose of this chapter is to provide you with the steps that you will need to begin flipping. These are hands-on steps. That means that these are steps that will actually require doing something, or at the very least to engage in a form of thinking that will help to facilitate your flipping endeavor. Some of these steps are intuitive while others may be a little different than what you were expecting. Here are some of the things that you will need to do:

- Make an analysis of your current financial and life situation
- Think about the sort of life that you want and how flipping can help you achieve that
- Make a list of the things you will need to do to prepare yourself for flipping
- Understand that flipping requires free time, capital, a team of workers, and a strategy

Analyzing Your Current Situation

Many of you reading this and embarking on a career in flipping do not have a background in real estate. Many will not have a real estate license, you may not have formal education in real estate, and you do not have more than passing familiarity with the economic trends that have impacted the real estate market and will continue to impact it in the future. Therefore, flipping really is your first foray into real estate. It is important to acknowledge that you may be a step behind some who have more knowledge and experience than you do.

What you need to do is to place thought into how you can prepare yourself for flipping. This includes the steps we mentioned above, which includes analyzing your current financial situation, thinking about your personal goals, and understanding what you will need to get started. Although flipping can be done informally by purchasing a property, renovating it, and then selling it with a real estate agent, most people who decide to go into flipping as a serious occupation will obtain a real estate license.

Understanding the life that you want is an important preparation step. You want to align flipping with your own personal goals so that this does not become just another 9 to 5 to you, but an occupation that you are good at and care about. You are more likely to be successful in a career that meets your interests so it is important to try and make flipping align with those interest, whatever they are. If you like the beach, perhaps you can focus on beachfront properties or condos. If you love horses, you can focus on properties with stables, horse farms, or other commercial properties that deal with the rearing of horses or equestrian sports. Part of what permits people to be so successful with flipping is that they can align their work with the things that they love. You should find a way to do this, too.

Of course, there are the practical concerns of what you will need to begin property flipping. Some of these things are discussed further in the next chapter, including the realities that come along with being self-employed, but these include most of the sorts of things that you would expect like time and money. Here is a shortlist of what you will need:

- A set of goals and a strategy
- Free time
- Capital
- A team of house flipping professionals
- To set up a business

Of course, you also need the knowledge and experience in flipping to be successful, but if you do not have this you can obtain it over time. For example, there is the 70 rule in flipping, which states that house flippers should not pay more than 70% of a property's after repair value (ARV). Paying more than this may be considered overpaying for a property and can increase your chances of losing money on the flip.

Chapter : 4

Looking at the Long-Term

One of the purposes of this book is to prepare you to obtain financial freedom through property flipping. Flipping is not the only way that fortunes can be made in real estate, but it has become one of the more popular. Here we look at how flipping, though generally centered on short-term projects, can be a long-term endeavor.

Many dreams of leaving their full-time employment and making an income from real estate sources passively, or at least with less of a time commitment than their ordinary job entails. The main form of passive real estate investing is an investment in rental properties, but since flipping can be less time-consuming this can also be a passive income-generating activity.

As you can imagine, the income stream in flipping is generated primarily from sales of flipped property. Therefore the income is only passive because the amount of effort or labor required to generate the income may be minimal depending on how you decide to go about your flipping endeavor. Flipping can be a full-time job or it can be a part-time gig. Here are some of the main concepts about flipping long-term that you should take away from this chapter:

- Earning income from flipping (and real estate in general) is about thinking about the long-term
- Making sacrifices in the short term is important to make big gains long-term
- Making risk-benefit analyses can be critical in success in flipping
- Learning to understand market demand and planning accordingly can be crucial

Some of you may be considering leaving your employment to pursue flipping. One of the purposes of this chapter is to give you an idea of what you need to do before you leave your job. No one wants to leave their job only to find that their financial situation was not as rosy as they believed it to be. It is critical that you have an understanding of your assets, debts, and obligations, and financial outlook before you commit to flipping as either a part-time, full-time, or passive endeavor.

Be Clear About Your Financial Situation

Laying out your overall financial situation is one of the crucial aspects of getting started in flipping. This entails more than a list of your bank balances, assets, and debts. It also means having a practical understanding of what your financial situation is month to month. In other words, it is important that you know what your monthly obligations (expenses) are. Some men and women who go into flipping thinking that their financial situation looks like X are surprised to find that they did not fully account for their monthly obligations so their situation actually looks more like Y.

You should analyze your household monthly expenses honestly. This includes expenses that you are responsible for even if they do not directly pertain to you, such as outlays for a spouse or children. This can include things like food, clothe, spending money. Essentially anything that you would be responsible for paying for you needs to take account of. It is important to do this before you commit to flipping.

To follow is a list of some of the assets that you would want to account for during your preparations for flipping. You want to make sure that you list all assets, including those owned jointly with others and those that you may not consider private. Some choose to make this sort of assessment with an accountant or financial adviser while others who are more confident in their financial knowledge often address this task themselves.

- Capital in the bank

- Capital in the form of investments (stocks, bonds, cryptocurrency, etc.)
- Retirement accounts
- Real estate currently owned for private use (including your house)
- Real estate for income (including rental property)
- Property in the form of partnerships that have real value
- Automobiles owned
- Movable property (such as valuable contents in your house)

Think about the assets that you would list if you were being asked to calculate your net worth. This is essentially what you are doing with this task. The point is to get a sense of your net worth at the present time. You also want to start thinking about which of your assets (if any) are capable of generating income. Of course, it is important to have in your mind if any of these assets actually might not be yours, such as a house you are currently paying a mortgage on. It is often a good idea to attempt this yourself even if you think you will need an accountant so that you have an understanding of your financial situation.

The next step is to get a sense of monthly outlays. This will entail listing everything: all bills or expenses that your pocket is responsible for every month. Some bills may not be charged monthly. You may have quarterly bills, or you may give money to individuals without a regular system. Keeping track of things like automatic payments made to your credit card or bank account is also important.

The step is to follow is to understand any new expenses that may develop as a result of a planned life change. This can include out of pocket health insurance, accident insurance, life insurance, travel expenses, mobile phone bills, the list goes on. You should try not to forget these as they not only will help you to enter flipping with knowledge, but they can also help you improve your financial situation later on if you need to cut unnecessary expenses.

This has been mentioned at other junctures, but hard to calculate expenses like food, coffee, gas, clothing, and other items that you pay with cash or card outside of bills should also be taken into consideration. Some may be surprised to find that they spend $50 a week on coffee. Understanding these sorts of expenses can be difficult. A helpful approach may be to list all of the things you buy with cash or card in a given week and then use that as a barometer to calculate respective expenses. You may find that you spend more than you need to on gas, coffee, or clothes.

Now that you have a list of assets, monthly outlays, and new potential outlays you are ready to imagine what your financial situation will be like once you start to flip. Presumably, you will be using cash or other assets to finance your real estate purchases. You also need to think about how real estate purchases may temporarily impact your assets. Indeed, if you were to lose money with a flip you would potentially worsen your financial situation not only in terms of lost capital spent on the real estate, but money lost from dipping into your cash resources while you did not have an income. For this reason, some people choose to have multiple income streams before they go the flipping route. Whether you decide that you do as well is up to you.

The main purpose of the aforementioned assessment is for you to understand your net worth and monthly financial picture, but it is also to help you to get used to being in the driver's seat when it comes to your finances. It is easy when you are working for someone else to get used to getting a paycheck and using that for the things you need, but when you are in a business like flipping then you are basically writing your own paycheck. You need to make sure that your bank account can cover the check.

Below is a list of some of the steps that will help you prepare for flipping by understanding your financial picture.

- List all of your assets
- List all of your sources of revenue
- List all of your bills (monthly, quarterly, or other)
- List or estimate your other expenses (monthly, quarterly, or other)
- List or estimate any new expenses that will accrue if you change your life situation

These are the minimum steps you need to undertake before you begin flipping. Some of you may already be in the real estate game or work as independent contractors so you may have this assessment already completed. It is important to get into the process of changing your financial picture mentally as your picture changes practically. For example, if you purchase a new asset or an asset increases in value then you should change your asset list. Although most people with enough capital resources are able to engage in flipping, this process also helps you figure out if property flipping is right for you.

Looking at the Long-Term

Property flipping is based on short-term projects, but it becomes a long-term endeavor for most people. The majority of men and women who go into flipping do not do it because they want to turn their $50,000 into $70,000 and then leave the business. Most plan on pursuing flipping as a source of revenue in the long term. Once you understand your financial situation you will understand how much you are able to invest in properties both in terms of purchasing property and renovation expenses. This is the first step in your long-term preparation for flipping.

With your knowledge of your assets and how much you can put down for properties

(and put into properties), you are ready to start thinking about your future in flipping. With any investment, it is important to understand where you will be in five years, 10 years, and longer if you stay on course. Real estate investing is a can of worms that requires you to ask certain questions. What follows is a list of some of the questions that you should ask yourself in order to better understand both your short-term and long-term picture.

- Do you plan on investing as a sole proprietor or going into business with a partner (or partners)?
- Are you able to sustain short-term losses on projects that do not turn out as planned?
- How do you plan on structuring your business?
- Will you contract renovation work to private contractors or will you assemble a team?

- If you do plan on assembling a team, how will you remunerate them?
- How will you handle recordkeeping and tax issues?

Once you have a basic sense of where you see yourself in five or 10 years with property flipping, you are ready to start learning from others who once were in the same shoes that you find yourself in now. In the next chapter, we will learn about some of the great names in real estate and how they made their fortunes doing basically what you plan to do.

Chapter : 5

Learning from the Greats in Real Estate

Anyone interested in business should learn the value of having role models and mentors in your desired profession. Although it is not always feasible to have mentors when you are just starting out, it is always possible to have role models who you study and whose example you follow. You will be able to look at the lives and examples of these individuals and learn from them: both their innovations that lead to success and their failures.

In this chapter, we will examine four figures of real estate and focus on the main points that can be taken from their lives. In reality, many Americans and others have made their fortunes in real estate, which makes the process of selecting just four to study difficult. There are many individuals worthy of study, almost as many people have made their fortunes in this industry. Although we encourage you to do your own research and to cultivate role models who best suit your own goals, we hope that you can look to these individuals as an example of what to do in the industry (and in one case, what not to do).

John Jacob Astor IV

John Jacob Astor IV was notable for having the largest estate ever appraised in the United States at the time of his death in 1912, and of being the richest passenger to die aboard the Titanic. Astor was born in Rhinebeck, New York to a wealthy family. His great-grandfather was an immigrant who had made a fortune in this fur trade. His father and grandfather were merchants who helped to cement the family fortune. His mother was a dilettante of the old New York aristocracy. Although John Jacob Astor's story is not a rag to riches one, his example illustrates some of the principles that underlie many of the great real estate fortunes in the United States.

At the time of his death, Astor's fortune was valued at over $86 million, equivalent to more than $2.2 billion today. About 70 percent of that was real estate, including several hotels that continue to exist today. Perhaps the most famous of these hotels is the Waldorf Astoria, still one of the most well-known American hotels today, more than 100 years later.

John Jacob Astor IV was not only notable for building and investing in hotels in areas that were on the make, but he also invested his money made in real estate in other ventures. He also had several patents in his name, which seemed to be almost a type of mania in the late 19th and 20th centuries.

His life shows that many real estate fortunes come from having a mind for things other than real estate. By being a pioneer in other fields like electricity and transportation, Astor was able not only to increase his real estate fortune but make his own real estate properties the center of the cutting edge. There are many lessons to be taken from Astor's life, but perhaps two stand out. One is that branching into several areas of real estate can lead to a large fortune. The other is that real estate can be a staging ground for a fortune built on several different industries.

Drew Scott

Drew and Jonathan Scott is Canadian brothers who have created a fortune based not only on real estate but on television. They are hosts of an HGTV television show called "Property Brothers", which has generated a number of popular spinoffs. Property Brothers is a property flipping show, one of several on HGTV, and it focuses on the twin brothers helping couples purchase a fixer-upper and turning it into a dream home. Although the goal of the show is not to resell the renovated home for profit, the knack of Drew and his brother in rehabbing properties allows the value of the property to be dramatically increased.

Drew and his brother Jonathan began their real estate journey by leasing a house in their neighborhood, renovating it, and then renting it out. They went on to purchase the house and sell it for a tidy profit, giving them an ROI of over 25%. They continued to flip houses until they became well-known in their communities. They were known to renovate as many as 15 properties at a time. Their strategy was to do minimal Reno's by themselves, a strategy which worked well for them. They started their own company, with two main offices in Canada.

They eventually branched out into television in 2011, creating a show that became the highest-rated on HGTV. As with the other names on this list, there are many lessons that can be taken away from the life and career of Drew Scott and his brother Jonathan. They learned the value of renovating properties as cheaply as possible, using a real estate license to save on commission. They also created their business with several offices in their native Canada, allowing them to turn their business acumen and effective strategy into a sizable fortune. Finally, they realized that visual media is an important part of a brand, and know with their television shows their real estate fortune is larger than ever.

Carlos Slim

The name of Carlos Slim is a fixture on Forbes's billionaire list. Frequently in the top spot, Slim has made his fortune in several areas including real estate and telecommunications. A native of Mexico, Slim is listed as the fifth-richest person in the world with a fortune of over $60 billion USD. Slim is so wealthy that his business assets are believed to account for 40% of the Mexican Stock Exchange. If that fact was not enough to give pause, Carlos Slim is said to account for more than 5% of the gross domestic product, or GDP, of Mexico.

Slim is mentioned on this list for two reasons. For one thing, Slim used one of the more important strategies in real estate to build his fortune. He also used his capital founded in real estate to expand his fortune in other areas. The important strategy used by Slim to help build his fortune is to buy properties cheaply and sell that later at a much higher price. Slim is an expert at identifying properties and companies at depressed prices. He often hangs on to them for cash flow or sells them at a great profit because they were undervalued, to begin with. This allows him to make huge profits with capital gains, while also expanding his spectrum of assets because he is constantly seeking and investing in undervalued properties.

Perhaps the most important lesson to take away from Slim is that analysis is an important step in house flipping. You should become adept at market analysis in order to determine which properties are undervalued. As a house flipper, you can renovate these properties and sell them. If you choose, you can even hold on to them until the market in that area gets even stronger: making profits from rental income in the short term and then selling for a large profit long-term.

Leona Helmsley

Leona Helmsley is a little different from the other names on this list. Leona Helmsley, before her death in 2007, was one of the most famous names in New York City real estate world. In addition to several hotels, Helmsley and her husband Harry owned the Empire State Building, 230 Park Avenue, and the Tudor City apartment complex across from the United Nations. Helmsley and her husband were known for buying apartment buildings and turning them into condos, which made them two of the wealthiest people in New York as well as the United States.

But this latter strategy is not why Helmsley's name is on the list. The "Queen of Mean," as she was known, was famous for her disregard for others. She was known to skimp out on paying workers for things that she had contracted them to do.

She even avoided paying the taxman, eventually being convicted of federal tax evasion. During her federal trial for tax evasion, she was quoted as saying in a now-infamous sentence: "Only the little people pay taxes." In line with her "Queen of Mean" moniker, Mrs. Helmsley evicted her daughter-in-law from a condo she owned after her son died and then sued her son's estate to get money back that she had loaned him.

So what is the lesson to take away from Leona Helmsley's life? There are two, actually. One is that it is very important to pay your workers and to treat them with consideration. Not only do you rely on them for your business's well-being, but their goodwill benefits you later if you ever run into trouble. The second is that everyone has to pay taxes, whether they are little people or not. Being negligent with the paying of taxes and with record keeping is a big no-no.

Chapter : 6

Learning from Your Mistakes

Learning from your mistakes is one of the key skills to develop as a property flipper. Real estate is an industry where mistakes will be made, and failing to learn from them can undermine even the most talented real estate professional. Anyone who is familiar with the biographies of great business leaders will know that they all had setbacks and disappointments. There is no great name in a business that has not made a mistake. What you will need to do as a property flipper is to begin a process of learning from your mistakes. Here we provide you with some of the biggest mistakes that you can make in flipping, followed by a summary of the major take away points.

Mistake Number One: Not Setting Funds aside for Unexpected Problems

It is important to keep in mind that there will be unexpected expenses in every real estate project. It is easy to make the mistake when first starting out of failing to set cash aside for problems that you were not anticipating. Perhaps you planned on purchasing a certain type of flooring, but that flooring is out of stock so you have to purchase a more expensive alternative. Maybe your Reno is delayed and you have to pay your workers for another week of work. Perhaps the most common problem is an unexpected repair that is needed for a house, such as a floor that is not level or a roof that leaks. It is a mistake not to calculate unforeseen circumstances when estimating your renovation budget.

Mistake Number Two: Paying Too Dearly for Properties

A common mistake that is made early on in a flipping career is overpaying for a property. This does not mean that you should set an arbitrary dollar amount of how much you are willing to pay for a property, but you should think about the ideas of ARV and ROI that were mentioned previously. You should estimate your return on investment at 20% of what you put into the house. Also, you should remember the 70 rule. It is not a good idea to pay more than 70% of the After Renovation Value of the house.

Mistake Number Three: Failing to Increase Home Insurance Coverage after a Reno

It is important to protect your investment if you are considering selling your property (or even holding on to it for a while). Your renovation project can add 20% to 30% value to the house, but most policies require that you insure the property for 100% of its value. This means that the house should be ensured for its After Renovation Value, and this should be done before you start your renovation. This is an important way of securing all of your hard work in the future.

Mistake Number Four: Failing to Make Contacts in the Industry

Real estate is an industry where developing contacts is very important. Your contacts will be the ones to recommend potential buyers to your house, extoll your reputation to sellers considering selling a property to you, and to help you when you are looking for affordable contractors for your renovations. You will not get far in house flipping if you neglect contacts altogether. It will be important for you to cultivate relationships with people if you want to be successful. The impact this will have on your career cannot be overstated.

Mistake Number Five: Not Selecting Contractors Carefully

Selecting the right contractors is critical in a successful flipping endeavor. In most cases, your contractors will be the ones doing most of the renovation work for you. Although some house flippers choose to get involved in some aspects of demo and renovation, it is unlikely that you will be doing all of this work yourself. Selecting contractors carefully allows you to save money on renovation work, both in terms of capital spent on necessary expenses and time saved (or wasted). Make sure to select the people doing work for you carefully.

Mistake Number Six: Pricing a House Too High

Your goal is a property flipper is to eventually be able to sell the house. If your house is priced too high on the market after you have renovated it, then you will not be able to find a buyer. This can lead to a downward spiral where a highly-priced house sits around on the market too long and never finds a buyer. This will then lead you to drastically reduce the price of the house and eventually cut into your profit, if not losing them entirely. Perform a thorough evaluation of similar properties in the area as well as the value you have added to your house when pricing it. Wishful or greedy thinking will not get you very far in house flipping.

Mistake Number Seven: Neglecting a Thorough Evaluation when Purchasing a Property

Buying houses affordably is certainly a good strategy, but neglecting to examine them carefully and buying them as-is can lead to problems. You should thoroughly walk through and examine the property before buying it if you plan to flip it. As part of your flipping work, you will be renovating the property so your expenses can shoot through the roof if there is work that is needed that you were not anticipating. You can avoid expenses later by being diligent about examining a property and predicting what problems or costs might accrue in the future.

Mistake Number Eight: Over-renovating a project

Over-renovating a project is a common mistake in flipping. What this entails is doing too much work on a project with the expectation that you will be able to sell it for even more than you previously thought. This can mean adding the most expensive stone and backsplash in the kitchen, or the most expensive flooring on both stories of the house. Although it is not wrong to put your heart and soul into a house, you also need to keep in mind that you need to sell it. Will you be able to sell a property that you have priced $100,000 more than other houses of a similar size in the neighborhood?

Mistake Number Nine: Not Paying Attention to Staging

Staging is the act of using interior design to properly identify the rooms of the house and make them recognizable and attractive to potential buyers. Staging also involves giving the house a universal appeal and not alienating prospective buyers. What staging allows buyers to do is to recognize them in the house. It is easy for flippers to focus their time and efforts on the infrastructure and catchy features of the house (like a shiny new kitchen or bathroom) and neglect things like the choices of furniture or art in the rooms.

Staging can be essential in selling a house so pay attention to it.

Mistake Number Ten: Taking on a Project that is Too Big

A project that is overly large will leave you mired in the much of lost time and unnecessary expenses. Sure, it may be the case that five-bedroom houses sell very highly, and that particular house you were looking at can potentially sell for a lot of money, but do you have the time and money to renovate such a large house? Perhaps the house is 80 years old. Have you thought about what other problems the house will have that you will have to fix? All of a sudden, the profit from that five-bedroom house is looking much smaller than it did initially if it remains at all. When you are first starting out, choosing a project that is too large is usually a mistake that you cannot afford to make.

The Role of Delegation in Real Estate Management

Many of the mistakes mentioned here can result from looking at projects from one angle and ignoring other important facets of the work to be done. What can help here is to have someone else walk through the property with you and help you in your decision making. This allows another pair of eyes to look at the property, and it may be these eyes who notice that those basement tiles look suspiciously like asbestos tiles, or that the temperature upstairs is much higher than downstairs suggesting that the HVAC might be a problem.

Another important thing to do here is to delegate. This can mean that different parties in the flipping venture have different roles. If you are working with a business partner, perhaps you both make the decision whether to buy, but one person focuses on working with the contractors while the other person focuses on deciding what the value-added renovations will be. Working in this fashion allows you to prevent mistakes and make the best use of everyone's time. Good time management and delegation is good real estate management.

Chapter : 7

Financing Your Real Estate Project

Fortunately, there are several avenues for you to finance your property flipping project. In this chapter, we will discuss the main avenues available to you as well as the main areas that you can target in order to cut costs. You do not have to use your own saved cash to finance your flip although many choose this route. The main sources of financing for flips include the following:

- Personal savings
- Bank loans or mortgages
- Lines of credit or home equity loans (taken on your property)
- Personal loans from family and friends
- Loans from the government
- Hard money loans from investors

Many of the general ideas that you have about purchasing property will apply here. In other words, obtaining a property for the flip is not too different from how you acquired your house. You most likely obtained a mortgage for which you paid a certain amount of cash down. The same is true here. The difference is that your goal with this particular purchase is to increase the value of the property as quickly as possible so that you can sell it.

Some of the important concepts for you to keep in mind during this process are listed below.

Adjustable-rate mortgage: Most mortgages have interest rates that remain constant over the lifetime of the loan, but an adjustable-rate mortgage changes over the lifetime of the mortgage. This generally allows you to pay less in mortgage payments in the beginning and more towards the end of the mortgage.

Appraisal: The value of the house. If you are securing a bank loan for your purchase, you will generally be required to have the house appraised before the sale closes.

Closing costs: These refer to the various fees that you will have to pay for aside from the down payment for the house. This can include taxes, insurance, inspections, and other costs that can run as high as 5% of the cost of purchase of the home.

Fixed-rate mortgage: A mortgage where the interest rate remains constant over the lifetime of the mortgage.

Pre-approval letter: A letter from the bank stating how much they will allow you to borrow for the acquisition of a property.

This will give you a sense of how much is available to you for a buy.

Types of Financing Available

There is no wrong way to finance your flip job. Many people first getting started in flipping begin by leasing a property and buying it later when their financial situation improves. You may decide to start small and finance your first buy with cash from your savings (a smaller project) and then as you acquire more capital through subsequent flips, you may decide to scale up to larger, more lucrative projects that you finance with mortgages.

How you choose to finance your forays into flipping is entirely up to you. The goal here is to review the different types of financing options that are available to you so that you have a better sense of what might work best for your goals. If you decide that your market niche is going to be beachfront or high-end properties then you may have to resort to mortgages, partnerships, or other financial arrangements that would allow you to raise higher capital.

It is also important to keep in mind that there are specialized financing options available to certain groups. First-time homebuyers or owners buying in depressed areas may be eligible for government programs that help them to finance their buy. These types of programs will not be available to everyone. So if you live in highly valued areas like Silicon Valley or the Hamptons then there may be fewer of these types of options to choose from. It is important for you to do your homework, though, as a little time spent here can lead to huge savings later.

To follow is a list of the general types of financing available to those interested in acquiring property to flip.

- Traditional mortgages
- Purchases made in cash
- Owner-financed purchases
- Commercial loans
- Home equity loans
- Partnerships

Traditional Mortgages

Conventional mortgages are the gold standard when it comes to acquiring properties in the United States. Everyone engages in this type of loan, from couples looking to purchase their first home to investors looking to generate passive income by creating a portfolio of properties. Mortgages have come a long way from their early days as a way for people to raise cash from the property they owned. Indeed, there was a time when some people were so-called "land rich" and "money poor." Mortgages were a way for such people to raise money by using a property they already owned to secure a loan from the bank.

Now, the reverse is true. A mortgage is generally used to acquire a property by using that property as collateral. A homebuyer who fails to make payments on property acquired this way faces foreclosure. Today, most people who own a property but need a loan use a home equity loan for that purpose (or a commercial loan). It is important for house flippers to remember that they also require funds for the renovation work so they may need to secure more than one type of loan. For example, a flipper may secure a mortgage to acquire the property and a personal loan to finance the renovation.

Purchases Made in Cash

Cash-only purchases have the advantage of sparing the purchaser from having to deal with all of the paperwork and hoops to jump through that come with a conventional mortgage. When you make a purchase in case you do not have to deal with banks in many cases, which for some people is an advantage. Of course, a purchase of a property in cash represents a more substantial investment in a flip than a mortgage would. For many, cash-only purchases are risky business and, to be truthful, they certainly are. If you have the cash on hand to make large purchases then more power to you, but for the beginner, it may be a good idea to make a smaller payout with your own money by financing most of your purchase with a mortgage.

Owner-financed Purchases

Owner-financed purchases are a neat trick that allows someone who is really motivated to sell to assist in the transfer of the property. In an owner-financed purchase, the money for the down payment on the house comes from the seller of the house rather than the bank, as is the case in a conventional mortgage. There are several different types of owner-financed purchases, including lease-purchase agreements in which the buyer leases the property for a certain period and receives the title at the end of the period. They obtain a loan to pay off the remaining value of the property after receiving credit for the rent they paid up to that point.

Commercial Loans and Home Equity Loans

Commercial loans and home equity loans are popular options for people looking to raise money quickly. A commercial loan may come with a higher interest rate depending on what your assets are. These types of loans are basically borrowing money from a bank or other financial institution much like you would borrow money from a loan shark or other person. In a home equity loan, the property that you own is used to finance your loan. Equity represents what you have invested in the property. The home equity loan is therefore akin to a second mortgage on the property.

Partnership

A partnership is a way to share the liabilities that you would otherwise be undertaking on your own. Therefore, you may only have to front half the money for a purchase rather than the entire sum. Also, you can share liabilities that come with the purchase rather than having to be responsible for these on your own. Partnerships are very popular in house flipping. Sometimes the partners are husband and wife teams, or sometimes the partners may be siblings. You decide who you want as your partner based on who you trust to help you with the decision making about you're flipping investment.

Chapter : 8
Choosing a Property to Flip

The property market is filled with potential houses and condos available for purchase, renovation, and resale. Experienced home flippers already have objectives in mind when choosing a property to flip, but new flippers will have to put some thought into choosing the right property. For some, the prospect of making this choice is an easy one as they already planned their first flip, long before they actually made the leap, but for others, this choice can be filled with uncertainty and angst.

When choosing a property to flip, there are a number of things to keep in mind. You should think about your goals as far as what you hope to achieve financially with your flips and how much time you have. This was discussed at length in Chapter 2 in the context of having a flipping strategy and establishing your goals. Recall that this includes tasks like deciding on the types of properties you would like to flip, honing in on a particular geographic area to buy in, making a time of how much time in days or weeks you have to devote to projects, exploring who will actually do the renovation work, and thinking about the desired return on investment, just to name a few areas.

In this chapter, we will help you work with your specific goals and your needs to help you make the right choice of the flip. Understand that when you are first getting started, you will not have a rhythm or a feel yet of determining when something feels right or feels wrong. An experienced flipper may be able to walk through a property and say, "Yes, this is the one," while a less experienced person may never get this feeling nor have difficulty seeing the potential on properties. Analyzing the market is another important aspect of making the right property decision and this will also be explored in this chapter.

Working with Your Goals

Working with your goals means finding a way to align flipping houses with your life and career goals. This may be difficult at first, but it should become easier over time as you become more comfortable with flipping. Recall that these are the bullet points you should keep in mind when setting your goals:

- Property types
- The geographic area of interest

- The ideal of average lipping timeline
- Working with tea or hiring contractors
- Working on one project at a time or multiple projects
- Estimating the desired ROI

These sorts of goals are important because they will dictate the type of property that you can buy. For example, if your ideal flipping timeline is no more than 60 days (8 weeks), then this may preclude you from flipping very old houses or may limit the type of work you would do to just kitchens and bathrooms, leaving everything else the same. The geographic area of interest is huge. You can choose your own neighborhood or another area that you are familiar with for flips. This may be a good idea as it would limit your range to areas that you are familiar with and feel comfortable with.

This is a good time also tor hearkens back to the subject of return on investment, or

ROI. If you're desired ROI is 30% or more, you should recognize that this is a very high number and you would, therefore, have to limit your potential properties to undervalued properties or those that would benefit the most from a renovation for other reasons. Properties, where there is a housing shortage, may also give you a higher return on investment, although this shortage may also make renovations costs higher as contractors are also seeking to profit from the low housing supply.

Analyzing the Market

Once you have a sense of the sort of house you want based on your goals you can start analyzing the market. Analyzing the market can mean different things to different people. It is perhaps best to think of it as analyzing where the market is headed both nationally and in your local area. This will help guide you in your decision making when it comes to making your first property buy and subsequent buys. Indeed, market analysis is defined as a comparative study of the market value of properties currently.

The current market value of a property is different from an appraisal, which is performed by a licensed professional. Market values can be somewhat fluffy, meaning that the weight that they carry can vary. This variability can be a result of fluctuating prices in a particular area or even an overestimation of what properties are worth in any given area. An accurate market value requires that the property be compared to comparable properties in the area, which some neglect to do well. For example, you may compare your own house to a house that recently sold of the same size, forgetting that this recent sale was a newer house that was located on a corner lot. Your house is older and needs some work so even though it is the same size it is not necessarily a comparable property. You may have to subtract a certain dollar amount from this relative property value to get a real sense of what your property is worth.

Analyzing the market can be used globally to determine whether flipping is a good idea in a particular area. For example, analysts generally say that areas where the housing values are very high, like Silicon Valley in California, are not good choices for flips because the ROI from flips in these areas would be very small considering how high the property values are, to begin with. Areas that are relative underprices, like Chicago, would generally be regarded as better choices for flips.

You should not let a market analysis deter you from your dream of pursuing flipping. Studies have shown that flipping is on the rise nationally with about 6% of all home sales in 2017 were flipped. This may seem like a small number, but keeping in mind that flipping is a practice that is designed to make a tidy profit and that the percentage of flips is growing every year, flipping clearly stands out as an endeavor that works.

Things to Keep in Mind when Choosing a Property

So you have performed a market analysis and are sure not only that this is a good time to start flipping, but you have also determined that there are a lot of millennials moving into your desired flipping neighborhood. The houses in this area also seem to be undervalued at the moment. Now you are ready to choose a property.

There are many things to keep in mind when determining whether to invest in a property or not. Although you can theoretically decide to flip any property that you can afford to buy, your goal is to maximize your profits from the flip so you will need to put a little more thought into it if you want to achieve this goal. For example, we have already discussed the goal of a 20% ROI and the 70 rule. Recall that the 70 rule states that you should not pay more than 70% of After Repair Value for a property. But there are other things you should keep in mind.

Do you want to travel two hours each way to the property you are flipping? Perhaps you should consider investing in a property that, if not in your own neighborhood, is at least nearby. Invest in neighborhoods where people are moving in large numbers and property values are increasing. Make sure to invest in properties that do not have major structural or other repair issues like asbestos. This is especially important when you are first starting out. Focus on repairs that add value to the property. Neighborhoods that have tons of amenities will be more attractive to buyers so you might want to use amenities to weigh your decision, especially when choosing between two or more potential properties. As they often say in real estate: "Location, location, location."

Lead Generation Strategies

Now would be a good time for a quick word about lead generation plans. Lead generation is a buzzword in today's marketplace as many business owners use lead generation as an essential cornerstone of their marketing. For example, a business engaged in home renovation projects may pay others for leads rather than spend large blanket sums on advertising to everyone. So this type of lead may take the form of someone knocking door-to-door and learning who is interested in home Reno's, with the business than paying these men and women on the street for the leads they generated.

Lead generation is especially popular on social media.

Lead generation in the context of house flipping would mean converting prospective buyers in your flipped property into consumers with a vested interest in your product. Basically, you can think of it as turning a potential customer into a customer who is likely to purchase your product. Lead generation is commonly done through websites that direct traffic in various ways. For example, you can show your flipped properties on a website and then turn the interested buyer into a client by having them sign up for a mailing list. There are many ways to make lead generation work for you. Indeed, thinking about lead generation can help you make targeted decisions about which properties you would be likely to turn around for a profit based on consumer interest.

Chapter : 9

10 Lessons that Can Be Learned from   Real Estate Leaders

In time, you will learn the sorts of skills and beliefs that will help you turn your house flipping dreams into something real. House flipping is not hard. Indeed, many people with little or no background in real estate have successfully pursued house flipping and done well with it. They are able to do this because they have found a career that they love and have managed to turn their talents into a passion. Such men and women also learn from their mistakes, correcting themselves over time to mitigate those things that can derail them from achieving their dreams. Because such corrections take time, in this chapter we provide you with lessons that others have learned to help push you on your way.

Lesson One: Correct problems as soon as they arise.

It can be easy to leave things for later, but this is a mistake in real estate, and it is definitely a mistake in house flipping. Mistakes that pop up should be dealt with as soon as they arise. This means that a leak that springs up during a Reno should be handled now, not a week from now. Questions or problems that are relayed to you should be answered and dealt with as soon as you can manage it. Getting better at this will serve you well in the future. For one thing, it will help you save money that you would otherwise have lost because you waited. Also, correcting problems as soon as they come will also help you develop the sense that in real estate, time really is money.

Lesson Two: Be persistent.

It is essential to be persistent in real estate. Anyone who is familiar with house flipping programs on television should get a sense of the persistence by which successful house flippers approach their work and their lives. If you really want a property, do not take no for an answer. Perhaps your first offer on a property was rejected. This merely represents an opportunity for you to come up with a better offer. Perhaps the seller seems unmotivated to sell. This is merely an opportunity for you to try and convince them. It is often said that a buyer cannot be talked into buying a property if they are unmotivated, but people can be talked into things by the right kind of salesperson. If you want to be successful in this game then you will have to be persistent.

Lesson Three: Spend your money on areas of high return.

A big mistake that property flippers can make is spending their capital on things that are unlikely to increase the value of their property. Bathrooms, kitchens, master suites, exterior renovations, and landscaping can add great value to a house. Adding a mudroom or powder room, or turning a garage into another bedroom: these are riskier Reno's that cost money and may not add value to the property. Your goal is not only to improve the house but to increase its value. Let's face it. Some renovations may cause the house to look better but may not necessarily add value. Learn to focus on those renovations that will give you a high return when all is said and done.

Lesson Four: Know when it might be a good idea to work with an accountant.

When it comes to financial matters, there is a lot that you can do on your own. You can form an LLC on your own and you can generally file your taxes on your own. But sometimes it is a good idea to enlist the aid of a good accountant. A good accountant will not only help you save money, but they can make recommendations that may benefit you in the long term. As we have seen, house flipping is not as a short term of an endeavor as it may seem at first glance. The goal of most people is to improve their financial situation over a long period, perhaps 10 or 20 years from now. An accountant can help you with that.

Lesson Five: Understand the strengths and weaknesses of your partners.

Partnerships are a dimension that it is important to address in house flipping. Enlisting a partner can benefit you in your house flipping venture, or it may come with some problems. In general, most flippers consider partners to be a good thing, but it is a good idea to develop a sense of the relative strengths and weaknesses of your partner(s). Perhaps your partner is good at dealing with contractors, but not so good at decision making. It will behoove you in the long term to take stock of this.

Lesson Six: Learn to tell a good investment from a bad one.

There is a sixth sense that house flippers develop about properties. They can look at a property and tell if it is a better sort of investment or not such a good one. Telling a good investment from a bad one is a sort of calculus; it involves performing an analysis in your head. You essentially look at all the costs and downsides of property and weigh these against the property's potential. It is really the potential of a property that you are interested in as it is this potential that you plan to turn into profit. The long and short of it is that a property with lots of problems and fewer problems is a bad investment, while a property with more potential and fewer problems is a better one.

Lesson Seven: Lead generation continues to be an important factor in real estate.

We live in an information age, which means that men and women interested in obtaining information about this or that have many avenues available for them to obtain said information, and they generally want that information now. In terms of house flipping, developing a website and a brand is a great way to generate leads. If you are familiar with house flippers from television, they all have a brand that is tied to a recognizable name or image. Think of Drew and Jonathan Scott from HGTV's "Property

Brothers." They have a recognizable brand and an image that consumers value instantly (being twins does not hurt).

It would behoove you to incorporate lead generation business. An easy way to do this is to come up with a catchy company name and invest in signs and business cards that display it along with your image. Perhaps the most essential part of your real estate led generation will be creating a website. Most leads in highly successful business come from the internet. This means that most of the prospective buyers of your flipped properties will be looking for houses on the internet. It will be smart not to skimp on attractive website design and maintenance.

Lesson Eight: If at first, you don't succeed...

"If at first, you don't succeed, try, try again" is an adage that most everyone could learn from. This adage is especially true in real estate. Anyone who has followed the careers of the greats in real estate will clearly see how few if any of them progressed through their careers without some disappointments. Disappointment is how we learn to make the necessary corrections that lead to success the next time around. Your disappointments are basically you falling down and getting back up again, and no one is able to make it through life without doing this, regardless of career.

In the case of house flipping, this adage means recognizing when you have made mistakes and learning from them. As we have seen, common mistakes include buying an overpriced property or spending too much on renovations. These are mistakes that, unfortunately, many people make. Sometimes mistakes like these can lead to losses (or break evens) on a property. These types of experiences should not deter you. These disappointments merely present opportunities for you to do better the next time.

Lesson Nine: If your business is real estate, it is a good idea not to purchase properties in your own name.

This is a very important lesson that can be taken from the men and women who have created real estate dynasties that persist right up to the present. Legal constructs like corporations and LLCs exist for a reason. When you go into business, there are certain liabilities that come with that business. You can potentially be sued and lose your entire investment. Having your flipping properties owned by a legal entity rather than in your name protects you from the risk that comes from holding property in your own name. It is always a good idea to mark a dividing line between your business life and your personal line, and this is an example where this division is not only ideal but essential.

There are many ways that you can go about setting up a company that will hold the property that you will acquire. One option is to incorporate, and it is a common choice. You also have available to you limited partnerships and limited liability companies. Limited partnerships have been popular because the Fed does not take the partnership itself, but the investors report their earnings and these are taxed. It also is easy for limited partnerships to raise money. You may want to speak with an accountant or do some more reading to determine if a limited partnership is right for you.

Limited liability companies have become very popular over the last two decades. A limited liability company, or LLC, combines the benefits of a limited partnership with the benefits of a corporation. Most of you with experience in real estate will be familiar with LLCs because so many ventures in the industry are LLCs. LLC pros include pass-through taxation and simpler compliance rules. Setting up a Delaware LLC is popular because of limited or no taxation, so you might want to research whether this is a good option for you and your business.

Lesson Ten: It is always a good idea to be clear on what the responsibilities of partners are.

A partnership can be a boon to anyone getting started in property flipping. Partners not only allow you to share some of the financial responsibilities and liabilities with another person, but they also give you another pair of eyes (and another brain) to help you when it comes to making a choice. Recall that even the choice of which property to buy and why is an important one that sometimes requires input from another person. A partner can help you with all this. Indeed, some regard going into business with a partner as a less risky way of doing business.

But partners can pose problems. In particular, issues can arise when it comes to questions of which partner is responsible for doing what. This can especially be an issue when a ball is dropped. Which partner was making sure that all of the contractors were paid on time? Which partner was responsible for having the property inspected? One lesson that can be learned from experienced house flippers is that if you plan on going into business with a partner it is always a good idea to be clear on which partner in the joint venture is responsible for what.

Chapter : 10

10 Secrets to Being Successful in Real   Estate Flipping

Every industry has secrets that can aid you in getting a leg up in the game vis a vis others who are attempting the same things that you are. There are lots of secrets in flipping, and it is often these secrets that distinguished the high earners from those that do less well. These secrets will be explored in a moment, but an example would be developing a strategy of how you market properties to potential buyers. Some secrets are of the general variety, such as personal qualities that will benefit you in this industry, while others, like cultivating a mentor in flipping, are more specific. Find a way to integrate these secrets into your plan for success.

Secret One. Real estate is cyclical so always stay on top of market forces and be ready for change.

There are many who are wary about investing in real estate. Such people know that international markets like Japan, and even some parts of the United States, have experienced overvaluation of properties which resulted in much-lost capital when the real estate bubble finally burst. It is normal in certain industries for there to be cycles of growth and retraction, and this is certainly true of real estate. For this reason, it will be very important for you to stay on top of the real estate market internationally, nationally, and in your area, if you plan to experience continued profits.

Why should you care about international markets? Well, what impacts other countries in Asia and Europe generally results in market issues in countries like the United States, as well. Indeed, it is common in stocks and currency trading to look at Asian markets as predictors for what will happen in the United States. Although real estate may be more resistant to outside rends because it is more closely connected to economic and demographic trends at home, paying attention to these outside markets can cause you to develop a feel for when things are not looking so good. What you need to do also is to be ready to adapt to accommodate a changing real estate climate. This may entail changing your house flipping strategy.

Secret Two. Find a mentor.

The right mentor can make the difference between a career mired in mediocrity and missed opportunities and a career characterized by continuous personal and professional growth. If one were to take a look at the industry greats who provide inspiration to others by their successes and their abilities, one will find that they generally had one thing in common: a good mentor. John Jacob Astor IV had several generations of family members to look to for advice in his forays in real estate and other industries, and Carlos Slim and Leona Helmsley also had figured in their life that we're able to guide and mentor them.

A mentor is someone who is easy to take for granted when they are around. Even a few words to guide you in the right direction can set you on a career path quite different from what you would experience were the mentor not there. And it might be helpful to keep in mind that one day you might be called upon to pay it forward and mentor someone else. If you are going into flipping but do not have a mentor, now might be a good time to try and find one. It may be as simple as a letter, phone call, or email to someone you admire. Making the most of this secret may be simple, but it is incredibly important.

Secret Three. Marketing is the key to flipping success.

Marketing is everything in today's world and, to be frank, it has been this way for a long time. Marketing used to be limited to television, movies, and print advertisements, but no businesses have to deal with the information age and all that means for getting their name and message out there. Marketing in real estate will mean informing the public who you are and what you do. The benefits of successful marketing are so great that it is impossible to overstate them. Marketing means the difference between a continuous stream of clients and a slow trickle that eventually disappears. Your goal is a continuous stream, and you will not get that stream if no one knows who you are or what you do.

A critical part of marketing is branding. Think of branding as McDonald's golden arches or the Trump name plastered on family properties around the globe. Good branding not only makes your company recognizable, but it allows people to have a positive association with your brand. When someone sees your name, face, or whatever visual cue is associated with your brand they should think about quality homes. This means that branding is not just about marketing, but also about providing a quality product.

Doing both will allow you to lead your business to unprecedented heights.

Secret Four. Having a good partner in the business can make a world of difference.

A partner can do more for you than merely split the bill. Your partner is sort of your other half in the business who can help you make decisions or see dimensions of a project that you did not see before. Perhaps this is why it is so common in property flipping to have husband and wife teams. Your partner is someone who you trust enough to help you decide on how to spend your money or to clue you in when you are going down a wrong path. A partner does not have to be someone you know. Indeed, some individuals seek out partners who already have a background in the industry, which allows them to contribute in areas where they as investors may be weak. Whatever you decide, understands that a partner can jumpstart your venture.

Secret Five. Establish a rapport with the buyer such that they believe that you are providing value.

Your goal as a flipper is not merely to make a property look nice so that you can turn around and sell it for a high price. Your goal is actually to add value to a property such that it merits the higher price tag you are asking for it. But you need to have a rapport with the buyer such that they do not see you merely as a salesman, but as who you really are: the person whose flip represents the value they were looking for.

Secret Six. Educate yourself in wholesaling before starting to flip.

Many individuals in flipping (and real estate in general) have a background in wholesaling. Educating yourself about wholesaling, or even doing some wholesaling on the side, is a good way to become more adept about flipping. Industry insiders believe that wholesaling basically allows you to become not only a better salesperson but someone who has an eye for value.

Secret Seven. Have a formula in your head for the maximum you would be willing to pay for the desired property.

This is an industry secret that is encountered time and time again. Sometimes you may walk through a property and know that you have what it takes to turn it around and sell it for a profit. The reality is though that what you are willing to offer may be less than what the seller is willing to part with the property for. When you are sizing up a property, have a sense for the absolute maximum you would be willing to pay for the property. This will allow you to be able to act on the fly and nab that property should the seller reject our first offer.

Secret Eight. Think of property flipping like a real estate investment.

Successful flippers should always keep in mind that they are real estate investors. What this allows the property flipper to do is to always remember that their purchases have a purpose. They are not merely fun ways to throw money around or to spend your time, but they represent your livelihood. They are an investment in your future and the future of your family. Remembering that you are an investor allows you to see ever flip as an important part of obtaining your future goal. As much capital as you may have, you should always remember that you have no money to waste. You can be assured that the men and women who have made millions in real estate think that way.

From your first flip to your last, everything that you spend your money on is an investment. From the lighting fixtures you pick from your first flip to the type of granite you choose for that brand new, upgraded kitchen, everything is an investment that should pay off in the future. Thinking this way prevents you from making choices for the wrong reasons. Sure those imported wood floors look nice, but are they an investment that you need to be making? Will they add value to your flip? This sort of thinking is sure to lead you to the capital gains that you expect from your property flipping business.

Secret Nine. Fake it until you make it.

Many of you going into flipping will be taking a tour in uncharted waters. Your experience in real estate may be minimal. Your experience in sales may be nonexistent. Now would be a good time to learn the old adage: "fake it until you make it." Once you have a sense of the steps you need to take to obtain properties and flip them, you will eventually find that you no longer have to resort to your notes or cheat sheets. You will eventually be natural.

Secret Ten. Have confidence in your abilities.

This is a secret that seems too simple to be valuable, yet it is the most commonly encountered secret in the industry. Other people can sense if you have confidence in your abilities as a salesman. If you are not confident in your flip, others will be able to detect that. You should learn to be confident in the decisions that you made because it may very well be this confidence that lands you the sale.

Frequently Asked Questions

1. What is flipping?

Flipping is the colloquial term for purchasing a property and modifying it for resale. Modifying the property can include superficial changes or serious renovation work. Properties are referred to as flipped because they are usually resold quickly for a profit rather than holding on to long-term which typically happens with real estate investments. Real estate speculation has long been a common form of investment, but turning over properties quickly for profit has become more popular in the last 10-20 years.

2. Why should I go into flipping?

Many people go into flipping because they are interested in real estate. Others go into property flipping because they have extra time on their hands and they see this pursuit as a workable way to earn extra income. Some people choose to leave their jobs permanently and work fulltime in flipping. There is no wrong reason to go into flipping nor is there a goal that cannot be realistically pursued and achieved with this type of endeavor.

Whatever your reason is for going into flipping, it is important to understand just what flipping entails. Although prior experience is not required to pursue a career in property flipping, some knowledge in this area does go a long way, as with anything else. Many people go into flipping who have a background in real estate sales, investing, or renovation and construction work.

3. I have seen shows on television about flipping. Is there a reason why flipping suddenly seems so popular?

Real estate has become a very popular form of investment. There are a number of reasons for this. Real estate by many as a safer form of investing than the stock market, currency trading, cryptocurrency, and the like. In fact, there is just as

much risk in real estate as there is in other types of investment, but the possibilities of making money quickly and reliably with real estate are often much higher than in other schemes. Real estate also requires less experience and technical know-how than currency trading, the stock market, and other areas.

There have been a number of shows on cable television about property flipping recently. In fact, these shows have caused flipping to become more popular and well-known. This type of real estate speculation has been around for decades, and because of shows like those on HGTV and other cable networks, many men and women consider pursuing this type of investment, more so than would have in the past.

4. Is property flipping a form of speculation?

Property flipping is a form of speculation. This just means that capital is invested with the assumption that various forces will contribute to profit. In the case of real estate, inflation increased population, and increased demands for housing generally cause property values to rise steadily over time. Flipping is a unique type of speculation because the profit from the investment is expected to be earned in a relatively short period, rather than years or even decades later in the case of other forms of real estate speculation.

Because flipping (like other forms of real estate investment) is a form of speculation, there is some risk associated with. Property values can fall due to economic downturns, natural disasters, and for various reasons. Other factors can contribute to reduced demand for housing, even over the short period of time that the house is being flipped.

5. Is flipping riskier than other types of real estate investment?

Because flipping is a short-term investment relative to other forms of real estate investing, some do consider it riskier than other forms of real estate alternatives. One of the advantages of flipping is that a well-done job should increase the value

of the property by improving the structure in ways that buyers can see. This is the reason why the potential for profit is very great at flipping in spite of the risks. In reality, all forms of investment in real estate come with some risk.

6. Can I start flipping if I do not have a background in real estate?

A background in real estate is not needed to flip although it definitely does help. What background can provide for the flipper is an insight into what properties to buy and for how much. For example, someone experienced in real estate will be able to tell if a property is overvalued for its area. They also would have an eye to detect if renovation work is needed on top of the work that was planned as part of the flip. Real estate experience really helps the flipper make informed decisions about properties. Of course, experience in renovation work also helps in estimating rehab prices and making cost-benefit analyses.

But anyone with a desire to learn about real estate can pick up the tools of the trade with enough aptitude to be a success at flipping. This book is designed to have an eye for real estate not unlike the well-trained eye of the experienced flipper. You will learn how to scout neighborhoods and properties for potential flips, and you will learn how to best use your capital in your projects to maximize profit.

7. How much money do I need to get started?

The amount of capital you need to get started in your flipping endeavors will depend entirely on what your goals are. As you can imagine, property values vary greatly depending on what part of the country that you live in and what type of property you are intending to flip. Any property can be flipped, including condos, so you can flip properties valued at as little as $50,000 or $100,000 or properties valued at over $1 million.

You also need to take into consideration how much you plan to put down for your flip and how you plan to finance the purchase. Many flippers choose to use cash for

the purchase of the property as well as the renovation, while others obtain mortgages or other forms of loans. Obviously, the disadvantage of obtaining a mortgage is that this financial tool is designed for properties that will be held on to for long periods of time rather than shorter investments. This does not mean that mortgages cannot be used for flips, it is just that those who have the cash to be able to afford mortgages or loans tend to do so. The long and short of it is that how much you need to get started will depend entirely on what types of properties you are looking for, what your strategy is, how you plan to finance your purchase, and other factors.

8. How do I finance my real estate flip?

One of the advantages of real estate investing is that there are so many ways to finance a buy. Of course, these financing tools exist because of the strengths of real estate as a form of investment. Many property flippers choose to finance all of the costs of the job without pocket capital, while mortgages, loans, partnerships, and other options can also be used. You may have to seek alternatives to out of pocket spending for larger or riskier projects so this is something to keep in mind.

9. Do I need to devote all of my time to flipping or can I still keep my job?

Real estate is a great source of passive income, which means that real estate investing gives people ample opportunities to keep their day jobs. Even in flipping, there is the possibility of keeping your day job. Some flippers are involved in doing rehab work themselves, which can be difficult if you have a full-time occupation, but if you do not plan on getting down and dirty yourself then you certainly can flip and keep your job. You will have to set time aside to interact with your team or the workers and to visit the property, but many property flippers are able to do this while still maintaining another job.

10. How do I know which properties to buy and flip?

Understanding market trends, niches, and your own goals are important if your goal is to be successful at flipping. Other factors that will influence which properties to buy include how much capital you have to invest, where you plan on investing, and the type of work you plan on doing to the property. For example, some flippers plan to be very detailed with their flips, investing large sums with a goal of a larger profit. Others may focus solely on kitchens, bathrooms, and external features of the house in order to flip it quickly. Your strategies and goals will work together to give your insight on which properties you should buy and flip.

11. What options do people have if they have renovated a property, but they have not yet found a buyer?

If you have flipped a property and that property has sat on the market for a while you should not lose hope. There are actually several options for flippers in this predicament. Your list price may be too high so it may be necessary for you to come up with a price that better suits the market. You can take the property off the market for a while and re-list it later. Or, if your finances allow it, you can take the property off the market longer term and use it as a rental property. Rental income is always a go-to practice in real estate when selling fails, and though this is not ideal in flipping because the magnitude of capital that is often involved it is always an option.

12. Should I start flipping on my own or should I embark with a partner?

The decision of whether to flip on your own or embark with a partner is a big one. In fact, the decision to invest on your own or to go about it with a partner is always a big one, regardless of what you are investing in. Anyone who has watched any of the flipping shows on television knows that it is not uncommon for flippers to work with a partner or even a team. The reasons why partners and teams are valuable in flipping is obvious. A partner or a team can actually help you do some of the renovation work if you plan on doing most of the work yourself. A partner or team can also help you with the financial aspect of the flipping project.

But a partner or a team can also provide other insights in flipping that are less obvious. A partner can aid you by giving their own take in decision making. They may feel that a project is priced too high for the neighborhood and is not a good choice for a flip. Or perhaps their opinion is that the house is too old and there are likely areas that require rehabilitation that you have not even discovered yet. A partner or team is another set of eyes, ears, and brains that can give you a new perspective on the project. Starting out, it is often a good idea not to go it alone. In this regard, flipping as a form of real estate investment can be somewhat different from other investments. There are risks that come with diving into the deep end of the pool without a lookout.

13. Why do some people seem to be more successful in real estate than others?

There are many opportunities to make a profit with real estate, but there are also many risks entailed. Although real estate is understandable enough to most that anyone can have a go at it, some people are more likely to find success in the business if they have a real estate background or have worked in an area that gives them special knowledge or experience valuable to real estate. So individuals with experience in renovation or in managing demo and rehabilitation teams would generally have an advantage, at least as far as flipping is concerned. But this is generally true for real estate, where those with special skill and experience often have a leg up, which can lead to greater success. Of course, we cannot leave out that some seem to have a knack for the business and just get lucky.

14. What does the decline in new housing units constructed mean to me as a property flipper?

Many factors impact the ability to move property in the real estate industry, and this includes the practice of flipping. There has been a decline in new house construction in the last few years, which has big implications for the real estate industry. One of the big implications is that there will be fewer units available for

people looking to purchase houses. Although this cannot be construed definitively as a housing shortage in the short-term, it may eventually become a housing shortage as the population increases and the pace of housing construction does not keep up.

The practical implications of this for house flipping in the short-term (and even the long-term), is that there may be an increase in housing values in the near future, even in the wake of fears that housing is overpriced in some areas. So your opportunities to make a big profit with flipping may be greater because of a reduction in new house construction as you will be competing less with new houses and more with older homes like the one you flipped.

15. What are some of the advantages of flipping compared to other types of investments in real estate?

Property flipping has become a popular occupation and pastime because it is enjoyable and can be highly profitable. The following is a list of some of the advantages of property flipping:

- Flipping is a short-term investment in which returns on capital can be made quickly
- Flipping is usually undertaken in the form of short projects where profit can be made over a period of weeks or months
- Advanced knowledge of real estate is generally not necessary in flipping
- Because flipping is a shorter-term investment, investors do not have to be concerned about long-term economic changes leading to a drop in property values
- Because properties can occasionally be bought with little money down, the potential to make large profits with flipping is great
- Flipping can leave those involved with free time to pursue other interests
- Flippers can choose where to invest their money in their projects based on their specialized knowledge and essentially function as their own boss

- Profits earned quickly can leave free periods in the year for travel, relaxation, or other forms of employment
- Much of the knowledge required to make money with flipping can be learned quickly

16. How is flipping different from investing in rental properties?

There are some similarities between flipping as a form of investment and investing in flipping. One of the big differences with flipping is that this endeavor can require more capital. Also, your success in the business can be closely tied to the knowledge that you bring in, how much effort you put into the project, and what sort of team you put together. Investing in real estate for rental properties can be a hands-off, passive type of endeavor while flipping tends to be more involved. Many flippers choose to involve themselves directly in the property rehabilitation, whether it be in the form of putting in new wood flooring, installing the brand, spanking new kitchen cabinets, putting new coats of paint on the wall, or handling the property landscaping.

17. Do I need other income streams if I am considering property flipping as a career?

Many people choose to do flipping as their sole career. This is a viable option for most as there are many options for financing flipping projects, allowing this to be a viable source of income for a wide range of people. Because having multiple income streams is a feature of the modern economic climate, some people who flip choose to have other sources of income merely to maximize the amount they are bringing in each year. It is easy to do this in flipping as you may have lots of free time, especially if you are contracting your renovation work out to other people. You do not need another source of income in order to flip, but you may decide that this is something that you would like to do.

18. What is ARV and why do I need to know about it?

ARV stands for After Repair Value. This is the value of the property after it has been renovated. It is based on multiple factors including the size and specifics of the house (number of bedrooms, bathrooms, etc.), and the going rate for similar houses in that neighborhood. You need to know about ARV because there is a common rule called the 70 rule in flipping. According to this rule, you should not pay more than 70% of the ARV for a house. For example, if the ARV for a house is $200,000 then you should not pay more than $140,000 for the house. If you pay more than this, you run the risk of losing money with the flip.

19. Do I need a real estate license to get started with flipping?

You do not need a real estate license to get started in flipping professionally although many make the decision to obtain one. A real estate license allows you to operate as a sales agent, leasing agent, or broker. There are benefits associated with obtaining a real estate license, including potential for more income, access to property deals you otherwise would not have access to, better education about real estate, saving money by not having to pay commissions, and creating contacts in the industry. You should weigh your long-term goals and needs in order to determine if obtaining a real estate license is the right step for you.

20. What is ROI and what should my ROI be in my flipping projects?

ROI stands for the return of investment. This is how much you are getting back on the amount you invested and it is usually given in the form of a percentage. So if you spent $100,000 and expect to get back a total of $130,000, then your ROI is 30% because you made an additional $30,000 on your investment. A general rule in flipping is that you should set your expected return on investment as at least 20%.

21. What are some quick flip tips if I want to sell a property quickly?

Although the goal is always to be as thorough as possible to add the most value to the property, there will be occasions where you are limited on time because you need

to sell quickly. Some easy things you can do are to clean the house quickly and make all the essential repairs, repaint all of the walls, give the landscaping quick spruce, replace the carpet in areas where there is carpet and there are no salvageable hardwoods beneath, install all new covers for the outlets and light switches.

22. What is a lead generation strategy and why do I need one?

A lead is essentially a customer who is likely to purchase your product. In terms of house flipping, a lead would be someone who is interested in purchasing a property in your area and of your type. A lead is on the step above a prospective customer. Indeed, a lead is generally conceived as a customer who has a high likelihood of buying the property that you have for sale. A lead generation strategy is a process of turning a prospective customer into a lead. There are many different ways to do this, but the internet and social media have become among the most popular because of the knack they have for spreading information virally. Your lead generation strategy should be well thought it, but it may consist of creative branding or coming up with a catchy website that draws potential clients.

Conclusion

House flipping is an art. It is a form of real estate investing that requires an understanding of nuances in real estate as well as the ability to make detailed and effective market analyzes. Real estate is an industry where there will always be a measure of risk, but house flipping done right can lead to sizeable capital gains. There is money to be made in flipping and as long as you have the right approach, you can do just as well as the many others who have made a go at this business before you.

Perhaps the first important thing is to recognize that house flipping is a form of investment. It is not a 9 to 5 where you sit in on your office cubicle and go through the motions until the end of the month when your paycheck comes in. In house flipping, you write your own paycheck. The paycheck you write is the result of careful planning, decision making, and hard work. How profitable your house flipping attempts will be will depend solely on you.

An education in real estate is one of the most important tools you can have when getting started in this trade. Real estate is still arguably the best investment you can make with your money. Housing is a basic need that everyone requires. Real estate is still subject to macroeconomic forces, but there will always be a need for families and individuals to have roofs over their heads. Education allows you to approach real estate the way industry pros do. In the first chapter, you were introduced to the real estate market today as well as other important aspects of the industry as the first step in your education.

Every investment that you make requires that you develop a strategy. Only fools spend their hard-earned or carefully saved capital on investment without developing a strategy. This is just as true of real estate investing as it is of currency trading or other investments you can make with your money. In the second chapter, you were introduced to the ways that you can develop a realistic flipping strategy and what that will mean for your future business.

Flipping is a pursuit that can entail large outflows of cash from your bank account. As no one wants to spend money without some expectation for a return, in the third chapter you were introduced to what you will need in order to get started in the flipping trade. It will take more than money alone. You will need free time, a partner or team to help you with your projects or decision making, an education in the trade and in market analyses, and, of course, a strategy.

The strategy that you develop should have a component of long term planning. Flipping is oft thought of as a series of short term projects that each lead to a profit, but if you want to be the best in this trade you will have to start thinking about long term goals. How does flipping align with your life goals? How much money do you need to make in flipping to be satisfied? How will you buck occasional downturns in the market to remain profitable? These are all components of your long term thinking that will aid you in this pursuit.

Fortunately, you have others you can look to when you are trying to come up with goals and strategies in real estate. Many fortunes have been made in real estate, and it would be wise to take a page from some of the greats who came before you. Strategies, like buying cheap and investing only in those projects that are sure to increase value, will serve you in the long run. Also, being conscious of the things you should not do (like failing to pay the proper taxes or keep adequate records) will also be essential in your success.

Another key to your success in this business will be learning from your mistakes. Everyone makes mistakes in every industry, and this is especially true of real estate. In flipping, a mistake can take the form of paying too much for a property or investing too much in the rehab. Even failing to stage a property correctly can be a major error. In the sixth chapter, you were exposed to some of the common mistakes made in flipping and how you can learn from them.

Financing is an area of real estate investing that most will have to pay particular attention to. There are some among you who are able to finance all of your projects with cash, while others will have to use the common tools of mortgages and government programs to finance their flips. Fortunately for the real estate investor, there are many ways to finance your flip, providing you with many options to engage in one project at a time or several. In the seventh chapter, you were educated on how you can use financing to get the best bang for your buck in flipping.

Once you have performed an analysis of the market, developed a strategy, and figured out how to finance your flip, it is time to acquire your first property to flip. This means that you must take all of the knowledge and planning you have engaged in thus far and use it to make an important decision: which house do I choose to flip? Many of you with a background in real estate may have a natural sense of what sort of property to buy based on your skills and your strategy, but for others, this sixth sense will come in time. You will learn to align your goals and strategies with every property you see, performing a sort of calculation in every house you walk through. This choice is an important one, and for most of you, it will become an easier one in time.

There are many lessons that can be learned from the great in real estate. Looking to others who have made their way in this business before you allows you to cultivate a mentor of sorts. These mentors have made all the mistakes and have learned the intricacies of the market, allowing them to navigate the occasional storms that come their way like pros. Although not everyone getting started is fortunate enough to have a mentor, all house flippers can use the lessons learned by others as their guide. It is a guide idea to look at the lessons that others have learned when you are feeling lost or uncertain.

Every industry has its tricks of the trade, and this is just as true of property flipping as it is of other industries. Some of these you were met with a few times in the book, like the 70 rule, or the 20% ROI guide. These industry secrets are designed to help you navigate the pitfalls that many new house flippers make. They also help you develop a sense in your mind of which properties form good investments and which are not so good. In time, you will develop your own secrets of the trade that you can provide to others looking to do what you did: make their way in an industry where there is money for the taking.

Property flipping is what you make it. You will get out of it what you put into it, so it behooves you to be as informed as you can before you even start. You can be sure that the greats in this business did find success without first understanding the secret formula. Your formula for success may be different, but when first starting out it may be a good idea to take a page from those who came before you. You will make mistakes along the way, but the well-educated investor is sure to make fewer mistakes than those who went in blind.